Redshift

2

© 2019 Respective Writers

All rights reserved for the author.
Please contact the author for permissions.

Arroyo Seco Press

Redshift Anthology #2

www.arroyosecopress.org

logo by Morgan G. Robles
morganrobles.carbonmade.com

ISBN-13: 978-1-7326911-1-7
ISBN-10: 1-7326911-1-8

for Michelle

Poems

4th Street	1
Balcony	2
"Minority poor" vs. "White People poor"	3
Miles to Sobriety	6
Walk of Shame	8
The Wish	10
Remythologizing	11
Peaches Three Ways	12
The Radio Signal is Her Only Guide	14
With Every Ache	16
She Still Smells of the One	18
My Grandfather Coughs	20
Beta Cancri	23
Carefree	25
Serendipity	27
The Beatitudes	28
Little Shell/Big Ocean: The Awakening	30
You've Got A Friend in Jesus (The Cross)	32
82 Miles from the Beach, We Order the Lobster at Clear Lake Cafe	34
Dear Dad,	35
There is no God	36
But I Hate to Keep Fighting with You	37
Limits of Hyperreality	39
Happiness	40
Afterlife	41
Shatter	42
Future Poetry	43
Exploring Comets	45
Mark Twain Probably Said It	47
Nocturne VIII	48
The Houseguest	50
Backyard Garden	52
Muse	54
Demeter Planting Strawberry Fields in the Nude	55
Letter to Ever Expanding Entropy	56
The Consolation of Ravens	58

Back Side of the Moon	59
Little Human	60
White Tulips	61
Dark Matter	63
If You Die in Your Sleep	65
Loki	67
The day the dreamcatcher backfired	68
Real Food	70
At Bay	73
Eclipse	74
The One Exception	75
Elegy for Roy Orbison	79
The Asteroid Interview	80
Fire	81
Until the Stars Collapse	82
No Stopping the Moon	83
countless summits	84
A Fall in Puerto Vallarta	85
For Love Alone	86
Saint John on Patmos	88
Driving Back from A Movie	91
The Middle of December	92
Seattle Waterfront	93
Double Rainbow	94
N.	95
State of Emergency	96
Atomic Space	99
Space Between	100
String Theory	102
Even Immanuel Kant Had to Do the Laundry	104
The Sacred Language of Wine and Bread	107
A Rainy Afternoon In New York City	109
I Am Fog	110
Náufrago Astral	111
Astral Castaway	112
Machine Dream	113
Meditations at the Verizon Store,	114

Redshift

the expanding universe
racing towards oblivion
in death or life

Suzanne Allen

4th Street
after Donna Hilbert

I was born in a valley—
foothills looming and
beaches beckoning—
I never wondered if I'd stay
or leave. My dreams
were of love
or so I thought. Freeways
unfurled like red carpets
in every direction.

In Alhambra, California
I am not yet nine months old.
My father leans over my crib
as the earth trembles—
some minor fault line slips,
rippling through our geography.
This, his memory, grounds
me, paints us in proximity—
always calls me home.

Suzanne Allen

Balcony

Two flies fuck on the awning flap,
less fuck than feed as they hang there
swinging upside down in the breeze.

The leaves rattle, having had their seasons
of sun and rain. The baby pigeons
are grown, have flown away, and I think

it would be nice to be animal like that,
taking flight when it's time, sharing
only DNA before buzzing off

into the bright of fall.

Lorraine Biteranta

"Minority poor" vs. "White People poor"

One small bedroom
six brown bodies.
Forgive me my rage
when you tell me how unfair
it was your parents only bought
one new game for your brand new
console when you were six
but when I was six
I was sleeping in a room
that only fit one twin sized bed
and one aging dresser
slept on the floor
in "Goosebumps" sleeping bags
with at least five other bodies
pressed tightly against mine.
Forgive me my rage
when you griped about sharing
a room till you were ten
but I remember
I shared a bed
until I was sixteen.

Lorraine Biteranta

When you were seven you said
you cried when your parents told you
they couldn't take you to Disneyland
for another year, "too expensive,"
and I bit my tongue, too ashamed
to admit I couldn't go to Disneyland
until it was free, and I was fourteen.
(Thank you, marching band.)

Please, forgive me my rage
when your parents couldn't afford you
those brand new clothes
that were "in style" in the early 2000's
but I only had clothing
once worn and torn
by somebody else.

And did I mention
mom was a smoker?
So my small hands
would cover my nose
whenever she was in

Lorraine Biteranta

but the room was so small
the stench the cigarette left
stayed embedded in the sheets
the same way the rage
embedded into my body
when you told me
you grew up
so
unjustifiably
poor.

I knew the word "poverty"
before I learned the word "success"
Forgive me my rage
you just wanted a new game
I just wanted warm meals.

Lorraine Biteranta

Miles to Sobriety

I can't take you with me when I go.

The mountain air will hurt your lungs
and you'll cough up thoughts
of meth amphetamine
from your last trip down.
I won't take you across the desert,
flashbacks of you on your back
sweating and shaking and overdosing
in the summer heat will tamper
with my memories. I won't take you
in the snow, not since I walked
in on you with that crimson stream
running down your nose. I can't take you
across the sky, past the same clouds
I touched with my eyes and my thoughts
when I flew over to find you
dying.
I can't bring myself to take you
anywhere we've been before.

Lorraine Biteranta

But the lake? I might be able
to take you there. We'll sit on that bench
and breathe in the colors the trees
bled for your survival, inject into our souls
the green grass and the clear lake
reflecting not just the trees, but the journey
I've seen—the miles you've traveled
to me, to sobriety.

Sobriety means
something new to you now. I know because
it means the same to me.

Lorraine Biteranta

Walk of Shame

Maybe it's time to walk away.
You would think that the first
purple stained splash of skin
would have given notice,
a letter of eviction written
the moment her hand
left a bruise under your eye.
You would think that maybe
after she asked you to lie
asked you to protect her image
and say it was an "accident"
you would read the signs
and leave.

They tell you it's hard to believe.
After all, "she doesn't look the type."
But, tell me, what type of profile
should predators, abusers have?
Does she have to be slender?
Does he have to be tall?
What scent should she choose
in the mornings,
what brand does he buy at the mall?

Lorraine Biteranta

Your feelings justify it all.
You forgive each time she raises
her hand, pushes you around
you can't stay angry long enough
to see the signs of destruction,
maybe you'll see it when it's late
you're too far gone
and it's too hard to create a life
without bruises and blood
so you can't walk away
you think you're sentenced
to stay in this
and when you get to that point,
you're gone.

Kelsey Bryan-Zwick

The Wish
"so I shot my horse
(poor critter)"
—Charles Bukowski

Wet denim skies, there a faint Orion arcs
over low-lying clouds, the almost fog
strung above lamplight, the ever present
harbor glow, and how the tallness of palm
trees becomes blind spot as you gaze up

What Bukowski wished for here
washed up from the shore, the same
salted air on his face, under the scruff
of his beard—nights like these, what
curses slipped his tongue, as he trudged

Maybe with a missing shoe, maybe
with a cat trailing him home, through
these alleys, maybe his pockets always
came up empty, like mine can, but if
only I knew, not even wild horses could
drag it away.

Kelsey Bryan-Zwick

Remythologizing

You are the ten stars the sky is anchored to
the hook to hang a hat on, the gestalt figures
drawn between spigots of light glittering

Everything in space is moving: no constant
vantage point, the Earth spins and orbits
the universe expands, and then there's us—

You though know this and shift from fish, to ram
to monkey; an expert dancer who wears one mask
and then the next

Over time, you shape these words, letter by letter
like a ouija mouthing from the unknown

The same phrase repeated
to love
to love
to love

As though the story stuck in medias res
loops, begins anew—begging resolution.

Kelsey Bryan-Zwick

Peaches Three Ways

One
Buy an extra peach, at least one
may turn between now and when
you have time to make the pie.

And please, no need to doubt the sun's
ferociousness, it is hotter than fire
hotter than laser beams, illuminates
our solar system without expectation.

Two
When you feel like an immovable
rock, let everything else be water
pushing away all your untidy edges
the stone-pit at the center of the fruit.

Today is neither good nor bad
like a peach grown, or grown moldy
it just is, and like this, you are also.

Kelsey Bryan-Zwick

Three
The day after my sister died, I found
myself in the Merrill College garden
under the orchard's canopy as I fed my
aunt and mother peaches, thinking *Huh*

Because I knew then, as I know now
*this is the best peach I have, and ever
could have tasted*: sun warm, fresh
seconds from the branch, my mother's
face, my aunt's.

Adrian Ernesto Cepeda

The Radio Signal is Her Only Guide

In a cul-de-sac as she pulls
over, her ears ring, guiding
like a bell through the night—
as her favorite Fleetwood Mac
song shivers in static, she's
already undressing you with
her softest eyes. From this
backseat rhythm you can feel
your *dreams unwind* seeing her
glow under streetlights, the song
keeps moving the both of you,
in unison, like tongues sharing
a microphone, and you two never
speak in words, only mouthing
verses like: *Would you stay if she
promised you heaven?* craving
every sound, breathing in her,
tasting every inch of her velvety
underground, she loves flooring
me while taking me places, I inhale
all her naked scents. *You've never
seen woman taken by the wind*

Adrian Ernesto Cepeda

through the rhythms resounding
speakers, she mouths *like a cat
in the dark…* you feel the marks
of her fingertips, on your back
like a needle hits a record, between
all the riffs, your blinking, feel
the spinning in her eyes;
you're instantly alive when
vinyl like she's grinding you
in circles; *and then she is
the darkness.* Sparking electricity,
clouding up the windows, deep
inside swallowing me in darkness
as she shares with you her
favorite part, between
the chorus and her whispers—
as the fade out comes,
devouring lips in her backseat,
hypnotically you are *taken by her sky*.

Adrian Ernesto Cepeda

With Every Ache
"My painting carries with it the message of pain."
—*Frida Kahlo*

Every muscle I move
my spine reacts—
immune, I wish there was
no pain, every year stretches
of skin and not just wrinkles
but every single bone becomes
less than brittle, just reaching
up causes spasms, feeling
like my back is haunted
by the most excruciating phantom—
just another throbbing, eternal
pounding refrain, endless wishing
no fear of a needle, give me
eyes squinting injection
for every one of my growing
afflictions. Even the carpet
stains mock me, constantly floored
from my back ceiling fan stares
dizzying me, constantly blowing
all my hot air. Restlessly I ponder

Adrian Ernesto Cepeda

dreading every tripping misstep
fall, my mistake—every glass
loves glaring back, shattering me
half empty, thirsting so many
contemplations, wishing I was
a bottle of Sauvignon, a cabernet
aging uncorked. Everyone would
sip me, instead of hearing each
wrinkled impression spewing
expletives with every cursing ache—
I regurgitate wine.

Adrian Ernesto Cepeda

She Still Smells of the One

Looking up with her telescope
eyes, she kept passing me her
bottle with so many mixed
messages inside, each sip
uncorks her cosmic
breath licked close, her curliest
of lips promising me our planets
we would glow so much
closer, it was like for this
one eternal moment her
heavenly body longed
for me, she was my mission
control, directing my lunar
landing—to me she tasted
like the one, but it was obvious
from the quiet between us,
the static distance, I was
just another Major Tom,
despite what *Transformer* sang
on my AM radio signaling
suggestive satellites, still
there was only simulation,

Adrian Ernesto Cepeda

she already drifting towards
another universe, her direction
focusing away from this
Space Oddity, in her mind
her supernova eyes reignite
already orbiting, telescope
focusing on another more
alluring galaxy, her Milky
Way longing for a distant
rendezvous—she was eager
to explore zero gravity
within someone else's stars.

Larry Duncan

My Grandfather Coughs

I

"I apologize for the color," he says,
and slaps the television a good one.
We've already opened all the presents.
There's nothing left to do but sit
knee deep in balls of crumpled wrapping-paper,
everyone balancing a plate on their lap,
searching for their own intimate space on the wall.
His hand rises to take another swing,
and a few nervous forks scrape
the last few crumbs of holiday crust.

The screen is a jump of jumble,
a storm of unseated tint and static.
The newscaster's voice doesn't fit
the pantomime of his mouth,
as if it was poorly dubbed in translation,
or thrown across some great distance.

He is saying something important,
something we all need to hear,
something about the weather
or maybe the president.
My God, has he been shot?
What if it snows?
And the children have no school?
Who will care for them?
Who will count their mittens?

Larry Duncan

And make sure that there are two?
My grandfather coughs,
and his heavy shoulders tremble.

II

Years later at my wedding,
my mother will push him in a wheelchair.
We will talk about the Navy, and I will remember
a photograph of him from World War II,
and how small he looked in uniform
packed in with all those other men.
The tubes from his oxygen tank
will fall out from behind his ears,
and dangle beneath his chin.
There will be music and lights
strung up in the branches of the trees.
There will be crumbs in the corner of his mouth
and dry spittle. I will reach out
with the sleeve of my shirt and wipe them away,
He will die while I am at sea.

My grandmother will still make pies for the holidays.
She will still watch television from a recliner,
and shovel snow from the driveway every winter.
She will close one eye and tilt
her head to one side as she watches,
as if peering through a keyhole.
Her skin will turn soft and blue
in the light of the screen,
and her head will hover

Larry Duncan

above her body like a cloud.
"Where do they put them all," she will say.
"after the reruns. Do they just disappear?"

I will not know how to answer.
Instead, I will remember
a time when I was a child,
a time when I crept
to a window to steal
a glimpse inside
my grandfather's workshop.
Board after board slides across a table saw,
sliced into smaller and smaller shims.
Sawdust rains down from the blade,
gathers in piles on the on the floor,
fills the air, confusing his face.
It hangs on him like a second skin,
like another body over his first,
a body of pale moss or fur,
a body he could shed at any moment
to become something else,
something terrible and true
like a monster in a story,
a story you might tell a child,
a story full of wonder and fear.

Larry Duncan

Beta Cancri

Walks home are the worst.
                                I can't keep straight.
      My feet always edge
                                away from even strides.

     My thoughts   like crabs click along on needle legs,
skittering over the body of Cancer,   etching an idiot story
       in cuneiform along the sand.
                             My father answers
      the concussion of copper wire,
  with a final convulsing strut   before the long muscle
                                    of the
                               body goes
                             limp,
bringing it flat with the earth.   What hum
                 did he hear?
    Learning to lie like feet,   one eye   covered in concrete
the other   staring wide
      through the mesh of wire,
                              seeing
                                the night
                                sky—

          not a diamond-studded shroud,
     not a network of veins
plied from a celestial body   and desiccated

Larry Duncan

                for display on black velvet,

                                          not luminous
        nodes erupting
                    in the final dilation
            of a dying eye,
—simply
the night sky

                                        and the terrible
t   r   a   n   s   l   u   c   e   n   c   e
                                          that cradles the
                      world.

Barbara Eknoian

Carefree

The boys, first and second graders,
play in the pool.
The six-year-old has to stand
on tiptoes to keep the water
below his mouth.
They place Styrofoam noodles
between their legs and pretend
they're riding horses.
Jordan floats on his back
dreaming up a game.
"Let's play you can be anyone
you want to be in the world."
Then he whispers in Tai's ear.
They both laugh.
I overhear "Tony Hawk,"
"Cat Woman."
Jordan says,
"Cat Woman isn't real."
Fate allowed them to be born
in mild, sunny California.
No need to alarm them
that the world beyond
their backyard is unstable.
The war in Afghanistan,
children killed in Syria.

Barbara Eknoian

They don't know the word,
hunger, as the children do
in Darfur or Malawi.
They row across the pool
on large tire floats,
splashing and laughing.
For now,
their juice and cookies
are set on the table
in the shade of the gazebo.

Barbara Eknoian

Serendipity

I waited my turn at the Serendipity Salon
in Teaneck, New Jersey,
for Michel, the French Canadian
to style my hair.
He charmed me, chatting feverishly
in his lovely French accent,
performing magic with his scissors.
I emerged feeling just like Jackie Kennedy.

He went south to seek his fortune
and there were always Michel stories
buzzing around the crowded salon.
He drove a Mercedes,
lived in an oceanfront condo
in Boca Raton,
and he was supposedly kept
by a wealthy Palm Beach man.

Until, one day, a patron announced
Michel had died from AIDS.
the stylists held their dryers
and combs in mid-air,
a woman interrupted
her sip of coffee,
someone turned down the volume
on the radio,
and there was a moment of silence
at the Serendipity Salon in Teaneck.

Barbara Eknoian

The Beatitudes

We are rounded up at the projects
by a Salvation Army team
who takes us in an old station wagon
to Vacation Bible School.
At 9 years old, it's the first time
I hear Scripture. When they recite,
Blessed are the poor in spirit
and *Blessed are those who mourn*
for they will be comforted,
I don't know what the words mean,
but it sounds beautiful to me.
When there's an altar call,
I don't know what it is,
but I feel an inner nudge to go forward.
I'm the only one in my group
to kneel at the altar.

Now, when I add a volume
of *The Best American Poetry*
to my collection,
which I've bought annually,
I'm troubled to see the first poem
refers to "The Beatitudes"
using vulgar slang
to describe a woman's anatomy.

Barbara Eknoian

Just like the day so many years
before when I responded
to the altar call,
I feel an inner nudge.
I sense it's right for me to rip out
the first page of my new poetry book
and tear it into little pieces.

Alexis Rhone Fancher

Little Shell/Big Ocean: The Awakening

1. Inside the shell: the girl. Almost 15, still submerged. She dreams ocean and desire until a boy swims out of her.

2. She's a bundle of suspense, her mother thinks. A handful. But the boy sees the girl, all her hunger. She has no mirror, does not yet know she is a siren.

3. Inside the shell: the girl. Her inner Mussorgsky. Her red bikini. Her demeanor a mediterranean pink, the color of her sex, libido - a jitterbug of stars - thrown against her sky.

She plots her escape. Tests the latches. Her mother tests them, too.

4. The family astrologer charts the girl's course. Venus in Scorpio. Her Leo moon. The foreseeable future? *Mars in the 6th house and invasion.*

5. The little shell drifts. Treads water. Her mother wants to keep the girl safe. But she is exhausted & works full time.

Alexis Rhone Fancher

6. Outside the shell: the boy. He's in over his head. His Circe is calling. The lure. The slosh and toss.

He buys a waterproof camera, infrared film to capture her.

7. The boy knows they are fated. Hard not to imagine jimmying the lock, their bodies colliding in the crashing waves, starlight, her briny coast glittering.

Alexis Rhone Fancher

You've Got A Friend in Jesus (The Cross)
for CMQ

You see Him at your bedside, glowing,
a nightlight of calm in an unsafe world.

Your parents can't help; they worship nothing,
while you sing hymns to Jesus in the dark,

bathe His bloodied palms in your dreams,
shudder at the cruelty of others.

At breakfast, when your mother asks,
you tell her you were practicing for assembly.

You wear a cross at school. En route, it burns hot in your fist,
but you fear your mother's displeasure, that she'll scoff

if you claim it repels the bullies who corner you at lunch.
Jesus protects you. He wants you to fit in.

Each day you pocket the cross before pick up.
"Just our little secret," Jesus whispers in your ear.

Sunday mornings, your parents sleep in,
you slip into the church around the corner, sit amongst the choir,

Alexis Rhone Fancher

delight them with your perfect pitch. You tell them
you're an orphan. They stuff you with parables and longing.

One afternoon you forget to take it off.
Your mother confiscates the cross.

Now Jesus can't find you on the playground,
but the bullies can, and push you to the asphalt,

your small palms bloody,
outstretched to break your fall.

Alexis Rhone Fancher

82 Miles from the Beach, We Order the Lobster at Clear Lake Cafe

The neon flashes "Lobster" and "Fresh!"
The parking lot is crowded. We've been driving since dawn.

The lobster must be good here, you say.

The harried, Korean waitress seats us near the kitchen.
She's somewhere between forty and dead.

I show you the strand of her coarse, black hair
stuck between the pages of my menu.

Undeterred, you order the lobster for two.

I investigate the salad bar.

Yellow grease pools in the dregs of blue cheese dressing;
a small roach skims the edge.

Before the waitress can bring the clam chowder, I kick you
under the table.

I'm sorry, I say brightly. *We've changed our minds.*
I'm responsible for the look of defeat on her face.

As I head out, you stop and leave a twenty on the table.

I have never loved you more.

Katie Sue Funk

Dear Dad,

Out of all the moments you were alive
I remember the moments I would dive
Into my writing because you said
I was farther ahead
than most kids
My age.

I was destined to write a masterpiece.
You said this was who I was meant to be.
Because
I was so stubborn,
I ignored you at first.

It wasn't until you died
That I realized
You were right this whole time.
While I was insisting studying science
Rather than writing,

You were trying to save me.
You knew me
More than I knew myself
And if I could have another
Word with you. It would
Be thank you and I love you.

Katie Sue Funk

There is no God

There was an adorable new couple
They were so young and frequently got in trouble
He liked it rough
They broke up
There is no God

Katie Sue Funk

But I Hate to Keep Fighting with You

You were watching TV
Which is your automatic
Response to a fight.
What you don't realize
Is that I don't hate
You. I love you.

You know you
Don't have to blast the TV
To ignore me. I hate
That. It's so automatic
For us to argue I realized
But I don't want to fight.

All we do now is fight
But I still want you
And you can't seem to realize
That. I sit and watch TV
With you. Automatically
I hate

How now the TV is now a punishment. I hate
How we fight
Over the stupidest things. It used to be automatic
For us to cuddle when you
Would turn on the TV.
Now I realize

Katie Sue Funk

Maybe you like to fight. You do realize
That I hate
This TV
Show. Yet, I still watch it during a fight
Because I still want to be with you.
It is so automatic

For me to get annoyed and it's automatic
For you to ignore me, I realize.
Maybe I am not good for you.
Fuck Grey's Anatomy! I hate
This goddamn show! I'd fight
For you to turn off the TV

But I'd hate
To keep fighting
With you.

Kathy Silvey Hall

Limits of Hyperreality

I stopped
Loving Disneyland
When they took the swans
Out of the castle moat.

They were the last pleasure
Not to culminate in a store,

The last lives
Among simulacra.

Alone among the fast passes
They floated, self-contained,
Unheeding of time.

Lights twinkle on.
Fireworks erupt.
Bodies are shaken and tossed
Towards experience, sensation, thrill,

But there remains no divine grace
Gliding
Unselfconsciously
Over the reflecting pool.

Kathy Silvey Hall

Happiness

I don't know if you remember,
But in my mind it is as golden
As a Ray Bradbury sunset
At the end of the last summer
Of childhood.

Where it was,
Why we were there
Could not matter less.

I can still feel the three of us
Running,
Holding hands in a row,
Whooping and yawping
In sheer joy.

More closely knit than I have ever been with anyone,
United, intimate.

We were,
Though no longer children,
Young enough to feel our power
To see the night new and clear.

We three, bright and fearless.

Kathy Silvey Hall

Afterlife

The film unspools,
Throws hot, sharp shadows
On the studio wall.

A stately Joy Division anthem swells.

Duck under the doorway into
The amethyst night
Cut open to reveal the crystal heart
Of promise.

I believed life was beginning.

How are we to know

How rare
Those flickering images
Those fading notes
Those beautiful faces and forms
Draped in momentary glow.

How seldom our hearts would open so breathtakingly wide.

How to release a promise of more
And hold all there is.

Brian Harman

Shatter

Shatter all myths about yourself.   Shatter
the years in the desert.   Shatter the whispers
in the wind.   Shatter the demons in the mirror.
Don't even bother   to bend   to pick up
the pieces.   You were already broken inside.
They will fall   the way   they were cut,
like crackled prisms   of an empty wine glass.
They will reflect   shattered   memories.
You will feel the crunch   under your feet.
You will get another glass.   You will smile.
You will pour.   You will tell a brand new story.

Brian Harman

Future Poetry

Particle I
Strap on your VR
helmet. Eye scroll
down to select
a category. There
it is, Poetry. No,
you passed it you
pervert. Not Porn.
OK, Poetry will
wait for you.

Particle II
Like a hot, lovely,
tongue in your ear
or the insertion
of Khan's eels.

Particle III
Satellite pings are
related to bongos
of the past. A turtle-
necked alien vapes
an O. It was poison.
It was beaten and
sputtered. A black
beret rests on the
hip of Rasputin.

Brian Harman

Particle IV
Oregon does not
resemble an organ
or a gun.

Steven Hendrix

Exploring Comets

We talked a lot about comets in 1986,
The year Halley's comet made its appearance,
As it did every 76 years upon completion of its orbit;
When the Challenger astronauts were assigned their mission
To observe the comet for six days and report back;
I learned of Mark Twain's comment that he'd come in
With Halley's comet and he'd go out with it, and then he did;
My parents took me out on the long-awaited date
To look up at the night sky in hopes of seeing the comet pass;
Without a telescope, and with too many street lights,
I saw nothing, but I felt, with something like faith,
That it must be up above me as I stood there that night
Hoping to glimpse such a rare vision.

And now I think of comets again,
Without having given much thought to them since,
Because it occurs to me that they are much like the soul:
Floating through cold, dark space, appearing
With a trail of light, then hiding from sight again,
As though to say "I was here in a moment of intense
Joy and ecstasy, of intense suffering and bewilderment,
And now I'm not."

Steven Hendrix

The child trapped inside me still from 1986,
Who looked up at the night sky with wonder,
Whose curiosity was not yet squelched,
Wants to know what has become of his soul,
What causes the light to burn so intensely,
And then become suffocated by gravity,
Whether it will take 76 years to return.
He's still awaiting further report from the Challenger.

Steven Hendrix

Mark Twain Probably Said It
"The universe of the mind is constantly expanding."
—Mark Twain

People are always saying these days
that sayings long assigned to Mark Twain
weren't really said by him

But what people don't realize
is that Mark Twain said so many things
in so many different forums

Even the things he didn't say

Steven Hendrix

Nocturne VIII

I bathe my thoughts
    in whiskey springs
            again

so I don't have to look
    at them directly

reflections of a warped soul
    at odds with itself

because something
    has become too much
            again

though the moon
    is still 252,700 miles away
            some nights

and my thoughts bounce
    off particles of light

that move through me
    in waves

Steven Hendrix

at 186,000 miles
    per second

all I need
    is to catch a glimpse

to find my way back
                again

Robin Hudechek

The Houseguest

My brother brought the tarantula home
in a glass box. You shut his bedroom door
and did not stop with the rest of us
to admire majestic mandibles
or furry legs nestled serenely under his body.

You did not watch the tarantula eat
or witness the drama of crickets flopping
in the corner of his cell, avoiding
the deadly stretch of arms
circling the crickets like a wicker cage.

The day the tarantula escaped
you hid under your covers
and stuffed towels under your bedroom door
only to awaken to black eyes
looking back at you with the depth
of a worm hole and the wisdom of an ant.

You imagined the tarantula nestled
in the folds of your blanket,
feelers tapping your bare toe,
fangs piercing your skin.
It didn't matter that you had blankets
or socks or shoes. In hot southern climes
arachnids and insects hide in sandals.

Robin Hudechek

Sending the tarantula to the garage was no solution.
Spiders preferred the warmth of car seats
and burrowed in the shadows of brake pedals.
But he never hurt anyone, we protested
as the tarantula climbed up my brother's arm.
He's not even poisonous.

Yet, even the cats avoided his cage
and the insects huddled in his lair
died slowly, perfectly aware
of the mandibles above them
a shadow closing in with the finality of night.

Robin Hudechek

Backyard Garden

First came the blooming of the forsythia,
newly drenched in sun and rain, tapping
our bedroom window and blazing yellow as
those humid May days to come.
The forsythia was a fitting awning for our clubhouse,
one branch blocking the entrance like a bright garland,
heavy with flowers we twisted into wreaths, proud crowns,
before admitting another friend to our sanctuary.

Next came the lilac bush in heavy clusters, a colony
of blooms, each floret an adornment for the fingertips,
and the spray of violet petals below.

The wild rosebushes budded in late spring,
thorns bristling like cat claws and dropping petals,
each one a magic carpet for lady bugs
and our whispered wishes.
We gathered fallen rose petals in sand buckets
and soaked them in water to make perfume,
ignorant of how to capture and preserve
their dying scent.

Robin Hudechek

My favorite, white peonies bloomed in mid-June
and lived no longer than two weeks. By then,
the Michigan ground had thawed every last breath of winter
from its soil. We took to the garden barefoot, reverently
cradling these flowers, bigger than my hand, that signaled
the end of school, the beginning of summer
yet were far too fragile to stand the humid blast of long,
hot days enlivened with popsicles that had to be eaten quickly,
the days when the garden and its clubhouses were abandoned
for cooler places: the neighborhood pool, and the beaches nearby.

None of us were home when my grandfather hired gardeners
to clip away those wild rosebushes and forsythia trees,
until nothing was left in the backyard
but an abandoned swing set and the garage.

Even the doghouse was torn down—our hiding place
from the whirr of imaginary spaceships hovering in clouds
and the burn marks of UFO landings in the grass.

Spaceships don't land here anymore.
The garden is gone now, the house sold to a new family,
but in moments of half sleep I can still hear
forsythia branches tapping at my window
with their gentle promise of spring.

Robin Hudechek

Muse

When the moon passes through
the darkest cloud
you can hear them gathering,
teacups clattering against saucers
and a faint aroma of sea flowers.
A wave curls on the shore and for a moment
you can see them dancing, these bejeweled women
and their tuxedoed men. They pay no heed
to the hollow-cheeked girl who watches them
whirling on the ocean floor. She has given
them the treasures of the earth: gilded tables,
chests overflowing with pearl necklaces, oysters still
yawning behind them, a bloodied trail of
lives lost, a ruby choker still warm from the neck
of a drowned woman, cast from the bow of
a sinking ship. Treasures none of them can bear to touch.

LeAnne Hunt

Demeter Planting Strawberry Fields in the Nude

I track the curve of jawline, of cheek,
of forehead furrowed
beneath windblown palms.
I am smoothing the hills, mapping
this landscape
with wayward fingers. I feel
the stubble of cornstalks,
the cool soil turned by blade
and sweat
and the solid rock of bones.
I am the blue
covering a beating warmth,
like the kinetic heat
from flapping wings.
I fall lying still
and rise
with frantic breaths.
I curl along edges. I steam
into view. The space
between our bodies
is an endless fertile plain.
I plow the clock
for next year's harvest. I watch
the sun blossom
and fling seeds
into arcing galaxies.
I am milky with want.
I am an hourglass
spilling sighs.

LeAnne Hunt

Letter to Ever Expanding Entropy

You always get the last word,
though so garbled,
no one perceives
your point.
To you, the victor,
go the spoils—
raspberries
two days
from the store,
a fallen tree
and autumn leaves,
my daughter's potato
eyeing me
from across the room,
a seagull's torn wings
outstretched on sand,
any leftovers
in Cool Whip containers
unsent letters
and memories,
lost socks and mates,
a marriage
and all its bedding,
outgrown tire swings,
an unused crib.

LeAnne Hunt

Most processes are irreversible
that way—
fundamental laws
of breakage.
The milk blinks first
at your stare,
and iron bleeds and bends
to your will.
Spines curve and chins fall
at your whim;
even clocks crumble
when you check their time.
Your kingdom will expand
randomly,
indefinitely until time
stops.
No one will remember
this end.

LeAnne Hunt

**The Consolation of Ravens
and a Sky Emptying of Empathy: A Cento**

Forbidden   to fly back after winter
for all fowl, you know
had failed. You wanted to fall,
the world's prettiest bomb. And the indigo
to smother under your wing?
Since blackness can be removed so easily
made men thunder
what I know about the species:
the bursting-forth gold flash arrival
of the oil-undone bird
You'll see us from everywhere.

Page 22 of the following books and author:
My New Job by Catherine Wagner
Hard Child Natalie Shapero
Incorrect Merciful Impulses by Camille Rankine (pg 20)
Wild Hundreds by Nate Marshall
Afterland by Mai Der Vang
Apocalyptic Swing Poems by Gabrielle Calvocoressi
The Endarkment by Jeffrey McDaniel
Transitory Myth by Sarah Elizabeth Miller
Carnival by Alyesha Wise
Land of the Free Portia Bartley
chapbook by Sam Sax (poem "I Can't Remember the Last Time I took a Picture of My Asshole")

Tamara Madison

Back Side of the Moon

I couldn't see him at first—
where were his arms, his legs, his torso?
At last, I saw his big round face,
head tilted, fond gaze directed toward
only us.
I have examined its phases:
Melon slice
Dragon's eye
Soft balloon rising through trees
Searchlight sweeping night's landscape
Nibbled cookie
Nail paring
Hook to snare clouds and snag the witch
Creamy glow to pull a howl from the throat
Night light glowing behind the pines
Pale cuticle in afternoon blue
and now, the secret underside, gray and guarded,
puckered hole like an anus
proving that there's a man up there,
a man's moon.

Tamara Madison

Little Human

Today on your birthday
I'm remembering
how we stared
into each other's eyes
all day long in our bed
at the hospital, bathing
for hour after hour
in the deep abiding love
that is like no other.
There was a whole
other world in your eyes,
a world I could not touch
or even see, this place
you had come from.
And now you were here
and I watched
the other world recede
like a tide as you breathed
our air and touched
our world and became
a most delightful of new
beings, a little human.

Tamara Madison

White Tulips

After a week, their petals begin
to hyperextend, flute outward,
their creaminess to pucker.
No longer shy, now they display
their golden centers the way
an older woman exposes
her opinions. The flowers boldly
show their confident beauty
to the world.

I, too, am proud to show
my hard-fought opinions,
my faded self to the world,
wrinkled neck and belly
like the puckers on the ghostly
tulip petals, the stone in my ring
an adornment I would never
have cared about when my hair
was sleek and golden, my knees
smooth, my eyes bagless.

Tamara Madison

The white tulips lean now
from their vase, each one
reaching in its own direction,
no longer content to rise
like a chorus straight up
but telescoping over the table
searching, petals flared.

Now do you see me?
they ask, yellow eyes intent,
gauging your reaction.

Tamara Madison

Dark Matter

I think of the universe expanding,
imagine a big net sack like the kind
old ladies use in Russia that start out
small and grow large to fit

the loaves of bread, cans of fish,
bottles of vodka, juice, milk—
all the items she can scrounge
on her icy trip home. The universe

expands like the heart expands,
to love every child you'll ever have,
to love everything you can love,
even after you're sure you can't possibly
love anything or anyone that much again.

I imagine the universe as a great big sack
growing ever fuller with the souls
of every living thing that has ever existed
in this world.

I think this is where we're headed
when the Earth tires of us—we too
will join the many souls in the vast sack
of the universe, become part

Tamara Madison

of the dark matter that moves its mystery
upon existence, bending light, spinning
galaxies, sending the souls of the departed
hurtling into our dreams.

Tamara Madison

If You Die in Your Sleep

If you die in your sleep
perhaps you dream
your moorings loosen,
feel your true ship thump
against the dock

become a balloon,
weights thrown aside,
ropes cut, bumpy at first
then deftly mounting
the sky's blue eye

soar high over
the green-patch fields
of the living, your own shadow
a small black fleck
edging the horizon

wake from that dream
and thread yourself like smoke
among the lives of your living
and see, at last, what was going on
all that time.

Tamara Madison

Perhaps they feel you brush
the soft armchairs of awareness,
inhale the comfort
of your spirit breath.

As you glide away
perhaps they tell themselves
of course it was not you,
was only the longing
for you, the keen yearning
to say goodbye again.

Betsy Mars

Loki

What makes me so happy
about the way a dog laps water
from the dish? Tongue slapping
liquid, and once quenched,
the excess flowing over slack lips,
the floor slick with spit. Loki grins,
black nose gleaming, triple dipped.

Betsy Mars

The day the dreamcatcher backfired

from a black hole dense with dream debris
it spewed out neverending falls from buildings
and bridges, a finger's width from hitting bottom,
shapes shifting in the shadows,
shrapnel flying, close escapes.

The final exam is today.
You've slept through the semester
and forget your baby in the carseat,
left thirsting on the side of the road.

A sinkhole opens up, its dark mouth swallows all.
A wolf stalks you, ducking between trees
you jump into bottomless lakes
which suck you down

unswimming, limbs flail—
you fail to outrun the car
barreling and careening
towards you, its brakes broken.
You turn and there's a monster

Betsy Mars

in the closet and everyone laughs.
You're naked
and pee your pants,
wetting the bed. The twisting sheets turn

into seaweed, strangle and suffocate.
No one can hear you, screams stifled in
the boiling chokehold of your broken mind.

Penelope Moffet

Real Food

"Free samples of Asian pears,
Asian pears—free samples—"
no better than any other pear
but ah tomatoes
Ohio earthblood
running down my chin—

Brown fuzz tinged with green
kiwis huddle in three bins
four for a dollar
hard little knobs but
"put an apple in the bag
they'll ripen faster—"
farmer's lore
no extra charge

"Grapes! Ripe grapes!
No sprays, no union,
small family farm
we don't exploit the workers because
we can't afford the workers!"
Probably lies but
so long since
grapes lay
sweetly in my mouth
forgive me Cesar—

Penelope Moffet

Bronzeleaf lettuce
greenleaf lettuce
romaine
cilantro
green onions
brown onions
earth apples
rainbow radishes
purslane
persimmons
parsley—
I'm promiscuous
at the Long Beach Farmers Market
Brown eggs
tidy in their crates
home from the free range
wait cozy by
the Justice Bakery pumpernickel bread

No one has artichokes this week
or strawberries
they blame god
or rain

Penelope Moffet

Black-eyed peas
bean sprouts
green peas
garbanzos
cook them slowly
with the overripe tomatoes
onion
garlic
chicken broth
a little thyme and basil
a few cilantro sprigs

Panhandler sidles up
eyes replete shopping bag—
toss him an orange

No time to waste
I have to hurry home
and cook for seven days

Penelope Moffet

At Bay

When sirens wail
the dogs in the temple howl.

Once Masons shook secrets
out in the basement,
in rooms with strange names
and walls painted like cities.

Now only the hounds
on the third floor know
what bothers the bricks.

I want to live
in a room at the top
and capture the chants
the dogs shake out.

In a room with walls
that almost aren't there
I could hum and fly.

I could circle this town
with my red-rimmed eyes.

Penelope Moffet

Eclipse

It all hesitates.
Here on the back porch
in air which cools for evening
even in July.

The mockingbird
brazening surprise
strikes the rail and flees,
seeing me here.

Slow time.
When else if not now
while the mockingbird cries
and sweet william cools?

Bill Mohr

The One Exception

*(Listening in on a dialogue between
a congregant of the Flat Earth Society
and a Puzzled Citizen)*

"Firing a laser beam, stationed
eight feet above the ground,
at a target an equal height
on the other side of the Salton
Sea, the Round Earth
Society (aka *fake science*)
claims the laser will 'descend'
towards the water. Any magician
can manipulate the curvature
of water's surface as easily
as I pour pancake batter.
My pancakes are flat.
and scientists are flat
out liars. If the earth is round,
why do we only see one
side of the moon?"

"But you do notice how it's round?"

"Yes, but it's a flat round.
Besides, don't change
the subject. We're not
talking circles and
squares, we're talking
flat and round. One is
true, the other false."

Bill Mohr

"And God designed it
flat because....?"

"Ah, you
won't get me with
the old "What's
the advantage?"
trick of rhetoric.
It's flat, maybe not
a flat flat, but
flat enough
to build round
things on. It's
flat as the belly
of a turtle shell,
which is rounded
on top, but that
doesn't change
the basic design:
belly-flat, and
I can't help
but notice how
you, Mr. Know-
It-All have a
round belly,
typical of
intellectuals."

Bill Mohr

"OK," I say, not
being one wishing
to prolong
futility, "I'll
concede that
99.9999
percent of
your supposition
is accurate."

He beams
Like a constellation
That just farted
In the face
Of a black hole,
"Yadda-yadda,
baby, look
who's best.

 "You're right,"
I say, "Saturn,
Jupiter, Venus,
Mars, are all
flat. The Sun
is flat. The one
exception is
the Earth.
It's round,
because God
wanted it
to be special,
the way
your logic is.

Bill Mohr

I'm not sure
why your deity
put colored rings
around a flat
planet or why
the rainbow is
curved within
a rectangular
sky, but if
it actually helps
to think of it
as flat, so be
its sprawl."

He calms down,
begins breathing
in unison as we
meditate. We
slowly age together.
Friends die. Close
friends die. No matter
how implausible,
every theory wearily
unfurls one fractured
truth: how grief gathers
at a grave, and flattens
itself forever.

Bill Mohr

Elegy for Roy Orbison

Soon lips and mouth contour
a face. Bigger and bigger we grow
but the ratio of the universe
to our size stays the same.

All of us feel it—a terrifying
littleness. Yet suppose there were
a limit—that all there was stalled
at Mars or Jupiter and nothing else—

not even nothingness—pinched that
impermeable limit. That would be
scarier. It's easier to imagine
existence as immense and so we do.

Bill Mohr

The Asteroid Interview

"Any remaining
ambitions, now
that you've been to
Grail Castle and back?"

"Find an uninhibited planet
To burrow into."

"Death wish" notation.

"You mean uninhabited?"

"I wasn't hired
the first time because
I was a speed reader."

Finally, as at any job
interview: "Do you
have any concerns
about our ethics?"

"Empathy, like candor,
is vastly overrated."

Shannon Phillips

Fire
for Stan

My son is 8 and hates
reading. He doesn't understand
the quiet alchemy of printed words
when mixed with the mind.

One day, he tells me about *Dog Man*.
Yet another playground testimonial.

On the drive home from the bookstore,
it is dark. He raises the new pages
to court the light from car headlights,

not yet knowing just how much light
there is to catch.

Tere Sievers

Until the Stars Collapse

It could happen tomorrow, I guess:
the whole thing blowing up but
what if, until the stars collapse,
we decided that what we do really matters.
What if a compost pile could save the world,
or one kind word could change a life,
what if we walk longer, drive slower,
plant a garden, eat less, pick up trash,
smile at a stranger, turn off the device,
hold our loved one in a warm embrace?
What if that tips the axis in our favor?
What if it doesn't, well, no harm done.

Tere Sievers

No Stopping the Moon

I travel with the moon
as it drops me into morning,
watch its light ascend
as it pulls me into night.
I know the moon can't stop
its rising nor the galaxies
their spinning.
I can't resist the dying
or the tumble into space.
But I can pick the lilies,
place them on the mantle,
I can fill the vase.

Tere Sievers

countless summits

after the stars undress
and disappear
notice the dwindle of dawn
the sun's noiseless outbreak
then the hot swagger
a vault
to the center
of a cloudless sky
'till the blushing bandit arrives
to steal the sun and
leave a bloodstained sky
the birthplace of night

Clifton Snider

A Fall in Puerto Vallarta
"Then shall the fall further the flight in me."
—George Herbert

"Pick up your feet."
Mother used to say.
"Clean your plate."
I do it to this day.

A cobblestone this afternoon,
A rush to cross the street,
Too soon and yet too late.
Gravity doesn't miss a beat.

Two-three seconds suspended—
No memory: I feel so small,
My touring ended for the day.
My body takes it all.

Two worlds collide:
My body is one with the street.
See how it bleeds: fingers,
Palms, elbow, knees, feet.

Two Mexican *hombres*,
Angels I would say,
My friends too, help me
On this unusual day.

—4 March 2019

Clifton Snider

For Love Alone
for Achraf

I

Poets and writers came
to Tangier and Marrakech
not for tagine-prepared
vegetables, lamb, chicken, sardines,
olives of every color and kind, dates,
mint tea, "Moroccan whiskey."
White pomegranates, oranges, yogurt.
No, they came for *majoun,* pasty hashish,
kif, magic mushrooms.

They came for boys, young men with
skin more alluring than liquor, with eyes
that opened doors into pleasures now
barely dreamed of but in the fifties and sixties
were epitomes of desire and love.

II
Every five minutes I fall in lust or love:
the camel boys of the desert
are divine, as is the view at night
on a sand dune of the numinous
Milky Way and the panoply of stars.

Clifton Snider

But I have come for him, my longtime cyber lover,
with a mass of black hair, exploding, shaved
on the side in the current fashion, commanding
masculine hair: beautiful—what other word is there?

He embodies all the clichés
given us by the ancient Greeks,
ideals Michelangelo appropriated,
the rich warm colors
of Northern Africa,
the living package that
wraps the waves of his hard abdomen,
the muscles of his arms and legs: all this,—
erastes and *eromenos*
the Greeks celebrated
and Michelangelo carved and painted.

All this and to thank me for visiting his country,
he draws my name in green & red Moroccan Arabic
and sends a picture of himself holding it, his face
the face I love, the deep dark eyes,
deep with the mysteries of a continent,
the wisdom of youth, the full, perfect lips
I cannot taste for fear of king & country,
of triples of soldiers & cops holding
automatic rifles on corners of Casablanca,
terrorists against those like us
whose only crime is love.

Clifton Snider

Saint John on Patmos

By the River Jordan
I saw the Holy Spirit
descend like a dove
& hover over his head.

I knew then I would follow him
to the end. We bonded in love,
inhaled the fragrance that comes
from a hidden heavenly marriage.

My older brother, James,
has been dead
these fifty years, martyr
to King Herod's sword.

I preached in Ephesus,
was sent to Rome.
There the Emperor
dropped my body into a vat
of boiling oil. By grace
my flesh was not harmed.

Clifton Snider

I was banished here
to the mountains of
the island of Patmos
in the deep blue Mediterranean.

In this cave my lord and lover
came like exploding
volcanic fire,
charging me to write his Revelations.

You, Prochorus,
my young apprentice,
with the golden hair
and the luminous face,
face like the face
of my lord, listen
to my story, how I lay
my head upon his breast,
my holy husband, when
at supper he blessed us twelve,
knowing one of us would
betray him in the Garden.

Clifton Snider

Of his disciples, I alone
stayed by the cross as
he hung in agony.
I stayed steadfast with his mother, Mary,
her sister, and Mary Magdalene.
He said to his mother,
"Woman, behold your son!" And
to me, "Behold thy mother!"
I took her to my bosom
until the day she died.

Come Prochorus, let us rest,
ponder the mystery
of God's creation.
My days are few.
I give you word
of the Apocalypse.
Pass it on until
my lord returns.

Kareem Tayyar

Driving Back from A Movie

The radio is playing the 19th Century Opera
"Hansel and Gretel."
It's the middle of Act II,
Which means it's the "Evening Benediction",
A mix of classical strings, folk melody,
And choral power so dream-like
That this formerly traffic-laden
Main street is now a German
Forest in early winter,
The green streetlights like neon
Breadcrumbs leading me home.

Kareem Tayyar

The Middle of December

There is so much pink
In the sky tonight
I feel as if I have stepped
Into an Impressionist painting,
Something by Monet
Or Alfred Sisley,
The kind where the cathedrals
Look like clouds,
The clouds like waterlilies,
And the waterlilies
Like floating hearts.
Get a hold of yourself, Kareem,
I say to myself,
But it's no use.
I've spent so much
Of my life daydreaming
That I'm no good
At anything else.

Kareem Tayyar

Seattle Waterfront

The fish fly back and forth
Between the hands of fishmongers.
Children marvel.
An old fortuneteller
Reads the palm of the moon,
And smiles.
There are stars everywhere.
I think of Ginsberg
Roaming these streets,
Dreaming of Rexroth
And Buddha.
On the other side of
The Sound winter undresses,
Baring her breasts
To the Great Fisherman.
I have never longed
To walk on water,
But I wouldn't mind
Being able to fly above it.

Kareem Tayyar

Double Rainbow

I am in the parking lot,
Paper bags in my arms
Filled with apples and strawberries,
When I see them,
Nearly vertical,
Rising into the clouds
Like multi-colored ladders
Upon which a boy
In a fantasy story might climb.
I drive home wishing
I was that boy,
And dreaming of the world
That might lay beyond
Those clouds.

Francesca Terzano

N.

When I am with you,
Your arms warm my body.
Most People want
Their Heart to speed
When they kiss their partner.
But when you kiss me,
My heart slows,
remembering to breath.
When I lay down
And you are next to me,
I can close my eyes
Falling asleep.
Because in that moment,
I know everything is okay.

Francesca Terzano

State of Emergency

On February 15th 2019,
Trump declared a state of Emergency
To build his ridiculous border wall.

At 7am no one starting their work day
At Henry Pratt Co in Aurora, Illinois
Knew a real emergency would occur.

A man came to work.
His name does not matter
Even though his name will be
The first one to be released.
The media will most likely
Plaster his name.
Like he is a celebrity.

At this moment,
It is unknown if he knew
He was going to be fired.
But after a meeting,
He took out his gun
And killed five people.

Francesca Terzano

Trevor Wehner
A college student
Set to graduate in May.
It was his first day
Of his internship
In human resources.

Clayton Parks
He was a human resources manager.
He graduated from the same school
As Wehner.

Russell Beyer
A mold operator and
Union leader. He worked
For the company for
20 years.

Vicente Juarez
He was a fork lift operator,
And stockroom attendant.

Josh Pinkard
He joined the company
13 years ago, in Alabama branch.
He transferred to Aurora, Illinois
Less than a year ago.

Francesca Terzano

A friend said he was a Christian
Who never had a bad thing to say
About anyone.

These are the names that should be
Plastered across the news.
These are the names you should
Remember.

All that Trump voiced was the
Police department did a great job.

The gunman was an ex-felon
And shouldn't have owned a gun.

Do you remember the news day
Of February 15th?
What do you remember?

K. Andrew Turner

Atomic Space

Wonder
   at the dark
         ness
beyond the light
   the in-between
space   surrounding us all

do they connect?
    or separate?
   make us one?
or many?

With the emptiness
    around
  let us rejoice
at our distinction
   and let us be happy
in our sameness.

K. Andrew Turner

Space Between

Something changed in you
when our eyes met for the first time.
For me I could see the stars,
how the heavens formed
and knew, too, the truth.

When our star-formed bodies touched,
we expanded to infinity and I reached
across the coldness of space
for a hint of warmth and you
let me, never connecting back.

Then you let go, and we came
crashing back. Your answer learned
and mine crashed. I fell back
into my old ways, to the blank
empty, drifting away.

You liked me more then,
when I was just an idea
in your head, not flesh and bone,
as if my very skin created
a big bang and the existence you had planned
for us went up in smoke and you
no longer wanted me.

K. Andrew Turner

It had been so long since I'd found
an anchor to hold, gravity to draw me in,
and in moment, that was gone.
I'm sorry I said I'd meet you.
You had been excited,
and now as cold as the space between.

In this new universe,
I was not who you thought.
I cannot blame you for that cold.
It burned in me for years
and still does.
I wonder then, at how you'll
finally let me know.

K. Andrew Turner

String Theory

Fall has moved in announced by clouds overhead. Birds
twitter, chirping their glee
while the striped cat stalks them.

Air so still and quiet, the whirr of a fan is enough
to damage the ears this late morning
on a gray day named after the star in our sky.

My heartstrings pulled too tight.
Can this moment linger to fill a lifetime,
 a soul so empty, vast enough to cover planets,
solar systems, galaxies, all universe with pristine perfection?

Orange fruit hangs on a tree not citrus outside a dust-frosted window.

Aching heart, aching strings, just a theory.

A branch moves in unseen air, motion so trivial
yet bespeaks the action of arms, tying plants
to our chain of life.

We are in this together, plant.
You and I, planets and dwarf planets
and midget planets and planetoids
and fiery objects blue and green and yellow.

Who will pull the strings attached to my beating breast?

K. Andrew Turner

Once, wondering the same thing, I collapsed
on grass in January's searing heat crying salt
and nothing has changed except dehydration

and the expectation of love. It has been lost somewhere
under a rainbow in a Kansas green sky.

If I love myself then by definition
won't the whole? Then I will pull my own
threads and cords and dance.

Fred Voss

Even Immanuel Kant Had to Do the Laundry

Frank may have finally had the great original philosophical
breakthrough idea
he's hoped all his life he would have
at 15
he discovered his father's Emerson book and read 50 pages
of Emerson
then he read *Philosophers Speak of God*
and marveled at Immanuel Kant's "antinomies of reason" chapter
where Kant showed that even though man could use his
reason to prove that God
had to have created the universe
he could also use his reason to prove that God couldn't have
created it
and as Frank drives he and Jane down Ocean Boulevard
he reviews
in his mind how he went on at age 15 and 16 and 17 to read
Camus' *The Rebel*
Nietzsche's *Thus Spoke Zarathustra* in which Nietzsche
announced, "God is Dead"
Husserl's *The Phenomenology of the Mind*
and poured over the 6-volume *The Encyclopedia of Philosophy*
in the High School library
stuffing his mind with ideas like being and nothingness
and the reason for existence and existential absurdity and
nausea and alienation
and epistemology

Fred Voss

and getting so excited that he underlined passages
throughout the encyclopedia
and made the librarian mad at him
and Frank grips the steering wheel and turns to Jane and says,
"You know,
I was looking up at the stars last night and it came to me
how do we know the difference between Order and Chaos"
Frank looks over at the profound and deep sea over the Long
Beach bluff they are driving next to
then back at Jane
"I mean
how can we say if the positions of the stars in the sky have an order
or if they have no meaning at all and are chaotic
I mean
how do we really know when chaos ends and order begins
maybe there's no such thing as chaos!"
Frank practically shouts
as he smiles feeling as profound and deep as the sea over the
Long Beach bluff
Jane doesn't bat an eye
but looks over at Frank and states very matter-of-factly
"Oh, you mean like that chaotic pile
of dirty laundry you make each week spilling coolant and
cutting oil on your shirt and pants

Fred Voss

at work and then dripping beans and salad dressing and clam
chowder all over yourself at dinner
and then the order you finally make of it washing the dirty
laundry and drying it
and folding it and hanging it up in the closet
each Sunday"
Frank sighs
and knows he'll have to go back to the philosophy drawing
board yet again
somehow doing the laundry
just doesn't seem likely to change the course
of Western philosophy.

George Wallace

The Sacred Language of Wine and Bread

Apartment 5, often empty,
hearts that are yielding
eventually thrive, rooms
to grieve in are also portals
to recovery, to contemplate
quis ut deus, who is like
god? especially in the
first three years of a
seven year cycle when
it is often the hardest
to face death and death,
rebirth and then death again,
easier to lift up the sword—
apartment 5, often empty,
yes a fine place to study
the sacred language of
wine, of bread, to listen,
to cross over to the other
side and wait and return,
arms wide as water falling,
arms wide as four new moons
in each of the cardinal directions
(each moon notched 11 times)
a place to face the darkness,
to be taken out of the dark

George Wallace

and returned to the light—
bread from fire, wine from
an earthenware jug, peace
from the terrible jaws of war

and a blackbird singing in the branches of a bald cypress, singing

'be generous…
be the good'

and who is like god? all this fighting,
all this consummation—

the perfect asymmetry of heaven and earth!

what flows in you flows through you

George Wallace

A Rainy Afternoon In New York City

I remove my coat
I take off my hat
I shake out my
umbrella, take
a seat at the bar
and place my dog-
eared copy of
'Heart of Aztlan,'
Rudolfo Anaya,
on the countertop.
Dear bartender
capitalism is a
sin and I am
transient in the
western world—
I have no nation
save you—the
solace of hard
places and open
spaces holds no
meaning to me
there is no man
woman or child
from Albuquerque
to New York City
who can make
consolation pour
from a tap like you.

The human geography of all the Americas cannot map my
current joy

George Wallace

I Am Fog

I am fog, fertile and slow. I am
water and wine, I ride on the wind
and I stalk the sky at dawn. I actually
pass through rock and soil, embracing
everything I touch, and claim the earth
for my own. Who says otherwise?
Oh you may say I cannot escape Earth,
well that's true enough - though who
on earth would want to? Earth, with
Its firm grip on Everything - grapes,
vines, animals, men; Earth, with its
pastures, parks and seams of gold;
its farm tracks muddled with spring.
Why, without Earth I would be lonely
as a star! That's why you'll find me
here, in the rivers where the great fish
go to spawn; here, in lovers' arms,
where human hope still grows; here,
at your bedroom window, looking in,
as free as dreamers' hearts are free.
Do I roam in your own dreams, child?
Yes! That's where you'll find me—
Or find me on the mountaintop
Where the snows of winter moan.

Aruni Wijesinghe

Náufrago Astral

siempre impaciente
te has adelantado
cometa fugaz

me has dejado atrás
en el sendero cósmico
de polvo interestelar

te persigo
alrededor de los planetas,
a través de constelaciones

me oriento usando
un puñado de tus estrellas
y un sextante hecho de tus huesos

los futuros astronautas
eclipsados por ti

Aruni Wijesinghe

Astral Castaway

ever impatient
you've gone ahead
runaway comet

you've left me behind
in the cosmic path
of interstellar dust

I chase you
around planets
through constellations

orient myself using
a handful of your stars
and a sextant made of your bones

future astronauts
eclipsed by you

Aruni Wijesinghe

Machine Dream

fiddle with the elaborate language apparatus
run screaming from its lies
worship a TV show
chant its sordid music & cry together

you will dream in tongues
trudge to their drunken time beat
live like a mad man
ask what it all means, but no one will say

yet juices still surge
recall when we drooled honey
smeared our skin
with a thousand purple petals
watched the bare waxing moon
and ached beneath its beauty

I whisper these ancient memories to you
through your mechanical fever sleep

Aruni Wijesinghe

Meditations at the Verizon Store,
after Robert Hass' *"Mediations at Lagunitas"*

All the old thinking was about
the romance of photographs,
completely unlike the new thinking:
all technology, ones and zeros,
pixels hurtling through space.

Today iPhone is synonymous with
the incantations Konica and Lumix,
the reverse mystery
of celluloid negatives traded
for a thumbnail scroll.
Selfies replace
carefully staged Sears portraits,
snapshot reality exchanged
for the buffed perfection
of Instagram filters.
We curate Facebook feeds,
edit our narratives.

In my teenage years we hoarded
drugstore reprints, artifacts
recording our fleeting youth,
spontaneous and imperfect.
These amulets protected us
against our own looming obsolescence.

Aruni Wijesinghe

Passed from hand to hand, we held on
to the edges, careful
not to smudge history.
Now epic tales are entombed
in cell phones' bodies,
every image a fingertip away
while technology leeches truth from memory.

Forget the magic of the runes
Fujifilm and Kodak
inscribed on the backs of our lives.
Don't wait weeks for memories
to return, tucked into dated envelopes
behind the Fotomat counter.
No need to tear up pictures of old lovers:
with one click they are exiled.

Suzanne Allen is a former interior designer turned poet and writing instructor. Her poems appear in print and online journals such as *Cadence Collective, Carnival, Crack the Spine, Nerve Cowboy, Pearl, San Pedro River Review, Spillway, Spot Lit*, and *Tears in the Fence*, with awards from *California Quarterly, Cider Press Review*, and *Writing in a Woman's Voice*. Anthology publications include *Not a Muse*, (Haven Books,) *Strangers in Paris*, (Tightrope Books,) *Veils, Halos and Shackles*, (Kasva Press,) and *Villanelles*, (Knopf.) She holds an MFA in Poetry from CSULB, coedits *The Bastille* and has two chapbooks: *verisimilitude* from corrupt press, and just this summer, *Little Threats* from Picture Show Press.

Lorraine Biteranta is really bad at writing bios. She spends most of her writing career dreading the bio part, but whenever she's asked for one she tries to embellish herself and make herself way more cool than she actually is. In real life, she just writes in a journal and prays that whatever she writes comes out decent enough. Hopefully she passes the test this time around.

Kelsey Bryan-Zwick is the author of three chapbooks, the most recent being *Watermarked* (Sadie Girl Press). Disabled with scoliosis from a young age, her poems often focus on trauma, giving heart to the antiseptic language of hospital intake forms. A graduate of UC Santa Cruz with a B.A in Literature/Creative Writing and a Pushcart Prize nominee, Kelsey's poetry appears in *petrichor, Lummox, Incandescent Mind, Like A Girl, Storm Cycle 2015, Eunoia Review*, and more.

Adrian Ernesto Cepeda is the author of *Flashes & Verses… Becoming Attractions* from Unsolicited Press, *Between the Spine* published with Picture Show Press and *La Belle Ajar*, inspired by Sylvia Plath's 1963 novel, will be published by CLASH Books in 2020.

Larry Duncan currently lives in Hermosa Beach, CA. His poetry has appeared in *Juked, the Mas Tequila Review, Crack the Spine*, and the *Free State Review*. He is the author of two chapbooks, *Crossroads of Stars and White Lightning* and *Drunk on Ophelia*.

Barbara Eknoian's work has appeared in Pearl, Chiron Review, and *Silver Birch Press*'s anthologies. She was twice-nominated for a Pushcart Prize. Her recent novel *Susie Once Again* is available at Amazon. Her poetry chapbook, *Life is but a Dream*, is published by *Arroyo Seco Press*. She is a veteran of Donna Hilbert's poetry workshop.

Alexis Rhone Fancher is published in *Best American Poetry 2016, Verse Daily, Plume, The American Journal of Poetry, Rattle, Hobart, Diode, Nashville Review*, and elsewhere. She's the author of four poetry collections; *How I Lost My Virginity To Michael Cohen and* other heart stab poems, (2014), State of Grace: The Joshua Elegies, (2015), Enter Here, (2017), *and Junkie Wife, (2018)*. A multiple Pushcart Prize and Best of the Net nominee, Alexis is poetry editor of Cultural Weekly.

Katie Sue Funk is writer and poet who is a feminist and loves to read work by other women. She has been published many times with *Literary Alchemy* and a couple of times with *Voices of Eve*. She currently lives in Glendora with her family and her adorable chihuahua, Russell.

Kathy Silvey Hall is a Pushcart-nominated poet, author, humorist, and editor whose work has appeared in Red Hen Press' *LA Fiction* Anthology, McSweeney's *Internet Tendency*, and *Chiron Review*. Her book of poems, *Herstories*, is published by Literary Alchemy Press. She teaches English at Santiago Canyon College.

Brian Harman is from Orange County, CA, hometown, Yorba Linda. He received his MFA in Creative Writing from Cal State University, Long Beach. Some of his poems have appeared in *Chiron Review, Pearl, V: An Anthology of Poetry* (Picture Show Press), *Nerve Cowboy*. If you see him around town, feel free to join him for coffee, craft beer, fine wine, or a shot of something good.

Steven Hendrix spent the majority of his life in Orange County and Long Beach. He currently lives in San Francisco with his wife Erin and son Langston. He studied literature at California State University, Long Beach for 10 years. His work has been published in *Chiron Review, Askew, Drunk Monkeys*, and *Cadence Collective*, among others. His first collection of poetry with Christian Lozada, *Leave With More Than You Came With*, is forthcoming from Arroyo Seco Press.

Robin Hudechek has an MFA in creative writing from UCI. Her poems have most recently appeared in *Kentucky Review*, and *Ghost Town*. She has two chapbooks: *Ghost Walk* (Inevitable Press, 1997) and *Ice Angels* (Silver Birch Press, 2015). She lives in Laguna Beach with her husband Manny and two beautiful cats.

LeAnne Hunt (she/her) grew up in the Midwest and now lives in Orange County, California. She is a regular at the Two Idiots Peddling Poetry reading at the Ugly Mug in Orange. She has poems published in *Black Napkin Press*, *Rabid Oak* and *Lullaby of Teeth: An Anthology of Southern California Poets*.

Tamara Madison is the author of the chapbook "The Belly Remembers", and two full-length volumes of poetry, "Wild Domestic" and "Moraine", all published by Pearl Editions. Her work has appeared in *Chiron Review, Your Daily Poem, A Year of Being Here, Nerve Cowboy, the Writer's Almanac* and other publications.

Betsy Mars is a Connecticut-born, mostly California-raised poet and educator. Her parents gave her an early appreciation for language and social justice, which her childhood years in Brazil reinforced. She has a bachelor's and master's degree from USC which she puts to no obvious use. A mother, avid traveler, and animal lover, her work has recently appeared in *Writing In A Woman's Voice, Sheila-Na-Gig*, and *The Ekphrastic Review*, as well as in a number of anthologies and *The California Quarterly*. Her first chapbook, *Alinea*, was released in January, 2019 by Picture Show Press.

In the 1980s **Penelope Moffet** lived in an inexpensive apartment in downtown Long Beach and wrote these poems while earning her living as a freelance writer, photographer and publicist. The apartment building is long-gone, replaced by luxury condos. The Masonic Lodge next door, celebrated in "At Bay," has also been converted into condos.

Bill Mohr is a professor in the Department of English at California State University, Long Beach. *Holdouts: The Los Angeles Poetry Renaissance 1948-1992,* was published by the University of Iowa Press in 2011. His most recent collection of poems, *The Headwaters of Nirvana / Los Manantiales del Nirvana,* is a bilingual edition published by What Books in Los Angeles in 2018.

Shannon Phillips beats herself up daily for not studying Arabic more often.

Tere Sievers, a New Jersey native, moved to Southern California in 1968. She learned to embrace its subtle seasons and set deep roots here. She says, *Writing poetry helps me see clearly the joys of a long life and teaches me how to survive its losses.* Her poems have appeared in *A Year of Being Here, Nerve Cowboy, Pearl and Silver Birch Press publications.* Her first chapbook, *Striking Distance,* is published by Arroyo Seco Press.

The inaugural winner of the OUT LOUD: A CULTURAL EVOLUTION'S Lorde-Whitman Award, **Clifton Snider** is the internationally celebrated author of eleven books of poetry, including *Moonman: New and Selected Poems.* The latest of his four novels is *The Plymouth Papers.* He pioneered LGBTQ literary studies at CSULB. A multiple Pushcart Award nominee in poetry and fiction, his work has been translated into Arabic, French, Russian, and Spanish.

Kareem Tayyar's novel, "The Prince of Orange County", was released in 2018 by Pelekinesis Books. His forthcoming poetry collection, "Immigrant Songs", will be published in 2019 by Word Tech Publications. A Professor of English at Golden West College in Huntington Beach, California, he is a recipient of a 2019 Wurlitzer Fellowship in Poetry.

Francesca Terzano grew up in the Inland Empire where she received her B.A and M.A in English. She also runs a very tiny press, Literary Alchemy Press. She also loves cats.

K. Andrew Turner writes queer, literary, and speculative prose and poetry. In 2013, he founded East Jasmine Review—an electronic literary journal. His full-length poetry collection *Heart, Mind, Blood, Skin* is now available from Finishing Line Press. He was a semifinalist for the 2016 Luminaire Award.

Fred Voss has published 3 full length collections of poetry with the U.K.'s Bloodaxe Books. He won the Port of Los Angeles/Long Beach Labor Coalition's 2016 Joe Hill Labor Poetry Award and has had featured programs on his poetry broadcast on National BBC Radio 4 in the U.K. and on WBAI Pacifica Radio New York

Poet, editor and educator **George Wallace** is writer in Residence at the Walt Whitman Birthplace, editor of Poetrybay, and author of 34 chapter books of poetry. Recognized internationally with the Naim Frasheri Award, the Orpheus Prize and the Alexander Medal, he travels worldwide from his base of operations in New York City to conduct poetry readings and lead writing workshops.

Aruni Wijesinghe works as a project manager for Affinis Labs, an award-winning social innovation firm that helps clients creatively tackle complex global challenges through entrepreneurship. She holds degrees in English literature, dance and TESOL. Aruni's poetry has been published in *Angels Flight – Literary West*, *Dark Ink: A Poetry Anthology Inspired by Horror* (Moon Tide Press), *V: An Anthology of Poetry* (Picture Show Press), and is forthcoming in *Altadena Poetry Review* and elsewhere. She lives a quiet life in Orange County with her husband Jeff and their cats Jack and Josie.

Acknowledgements

Carefree published in *Newversenews*

Serendipity published in Barbara Eknoian's chapbook, *Jerkumstances*

The Beatitudes published in Barbara Eknoian's book, *Why I Miss New Jersey*

Little Shell/Big Ocean: The Awakening Published in *Rag Queen Periodical*, 2017

You've Got A Friend in Jesus (The Cross) published in *ONE JACAR*, 2017

82 Miles From the Beach, We Order The Lobster At Clear Lake Café published in *Slipstream*, 2017

Eclipse published in *A.K.A. Poetry*, Spring 1987.

At Bay published as a broadside by *Art Dog* in Spring 1988.

Elegy for Roy Orbison appeared in *Sonora Review* early 1990s

The Asteroid Interview appeared in *poeticdiversity*

String Theory appeared in a previous version in the art show *Me Small, Space Big* at Citrus College April 2012

www.ingramcontent.com/pod-product-compliance
Lightning Source LLC
Chambersburg PA
CBHW060159050426
42446CB00013B/2903